Panda-Monium

PANDA RESCUE!

T0020174

By James Buckley Jr.

Illustrated by Kerstin LaCross

BEARPORT
PUBLISHING

Minneapolis, Minnesota

BEAR CLAW

Credits

Interior coloring by Jon Siruno.
Interior inks by Haley Boros.
Photos: 22T © Kyodo/AP Images, 22B © Kent Gilbert/AP Images.

Bearport Publishing
Minneapolis, MN
President: Jen Jenson
Director of Product Development: Spencer Brinker
Editor: Allison Juda

Produced by Shoreline Publishing Group LLC
Santa Barbara, California
Designer: Patty Kelley
Editorial Director: James Buckley Jr.

DISCLAIMER: This graphic story is a dramatization based on true events. It is intended to give the reader a sense of the narrative rather than a presentation of actual details as they occurred.

Library of Congress Cataloging-in-Publication Data

Names: Buckley, James, Jr., 1963- author. | LaCross, Kerstin, 1988-
  illustrator.
Title: Panda-monium : panda rescue! / by James Buckley Jr. ; illustrated
  by, Kerstin LaCross.
Description: Bear claw books. | Minneapolis, Minnesota : Bearport
  Publishing, 2021. | Series: Rescued! Animal escapes | Includes
  bibliographical references and index.
Identifiers: LCCN 2020035456 (print) | LCCN 2020035457 (ebook) | ISBN
  9781647476199 (library binding) | ISBN 9781647476267 (paperback) | ISBN
  9781647476335 (ebook)
Subjects: LCSH: Pandas—China—Juvenile literature. | Wildlife
  rescue—China—Juvenile literature. | Wildlife
  rehabilitation—China—Juvenile literature. |
  Earthquakes—China—Juvenile literature.
Classification: LCC QL795.P18 B83 2021 (print) | LCC QL795.P18 (ebook) |
  DDC 599.7890951—dc23
LC record available at https://lccn.loc.gov/2020035456
LC ebook record available at https://lccn.loc.gov/2020035457

For more information, write to Bearport Publishing, 5357 Penn Avenue South, Minneapolis, MN 55419. Printed in the United States of America.

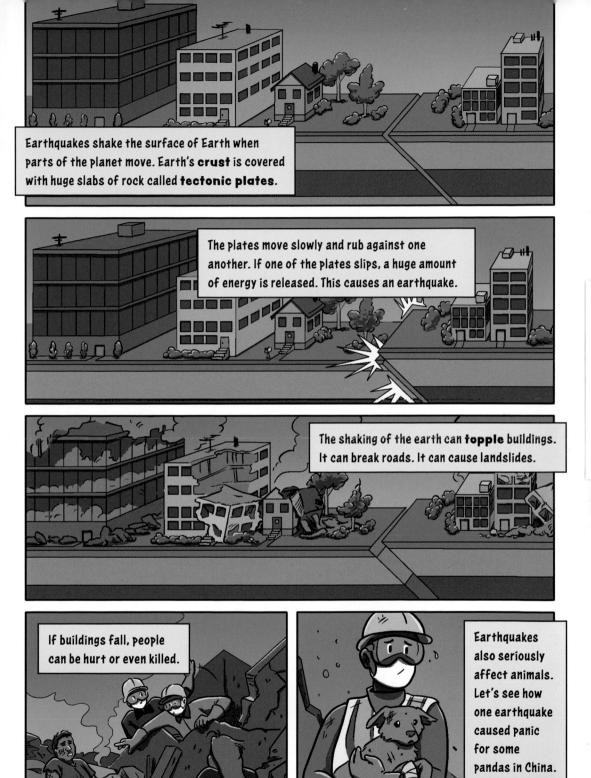

Earthquakes shake the surface of Earth when parts of the planet move. Earth's **crust** is covered with huge slabs of rock called **tectonic plates**.

The plates move slowly and rub against one another. If one of the plates slips, a huge amount of energy is released. This causes an earthquake.

The shaking of the earth can **topple** buildings. It can break roads. It can cause landslides.

If buildings fall, people can be hurt or even killed.

Earthquakes also seriously affect animals. Let's see how one earthquake caused panic for some pandas in China.

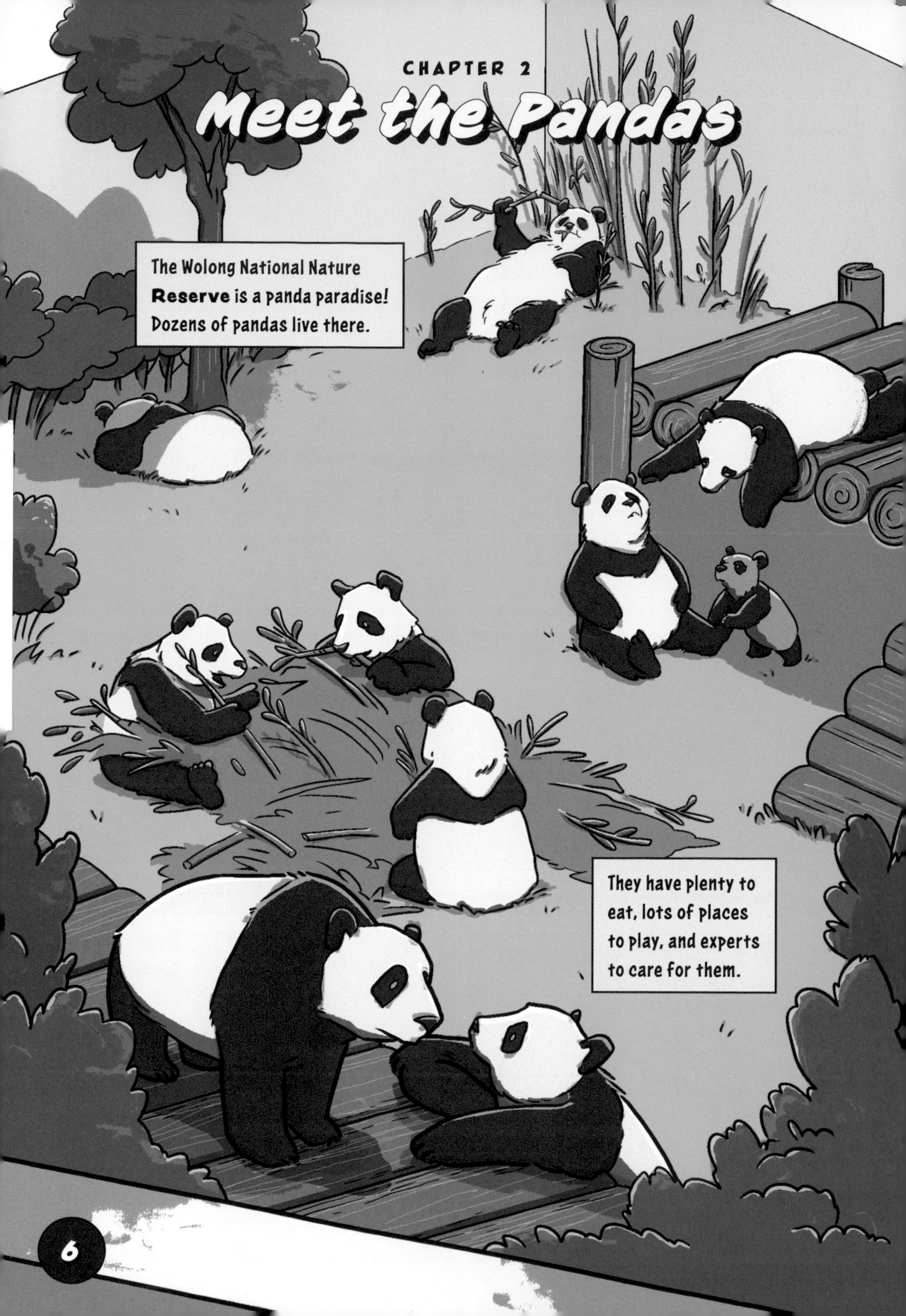

CHAPTER 2
Meet the Pandas
The Wolong National Nature Reserve is a panda paradise! Dozens of pandas live there.
They have plenty to eat, lots of places to play, and experts to care for them.

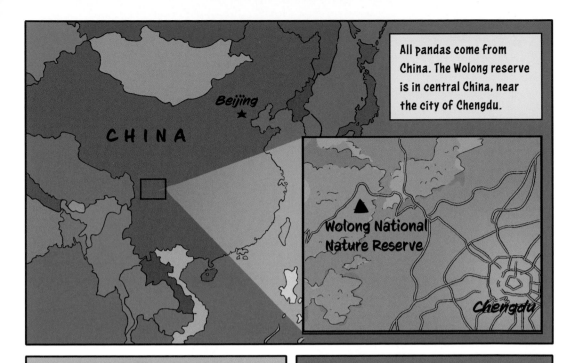

All pandas come from China. The Wolong reserve is in central China, near the city of Chengdu.

CHINA

Beijing

Wolong National Nature Reserve

Chengdu

But why do pandas need a safe place, such as the reserve? Because pandas are **endangered**. There are fewer than 2,000 of these creatures left in the world.

The Chinese government wants to make sure these famous animals stay around for the future. In the reserve, the pandas are protected and well cared for.

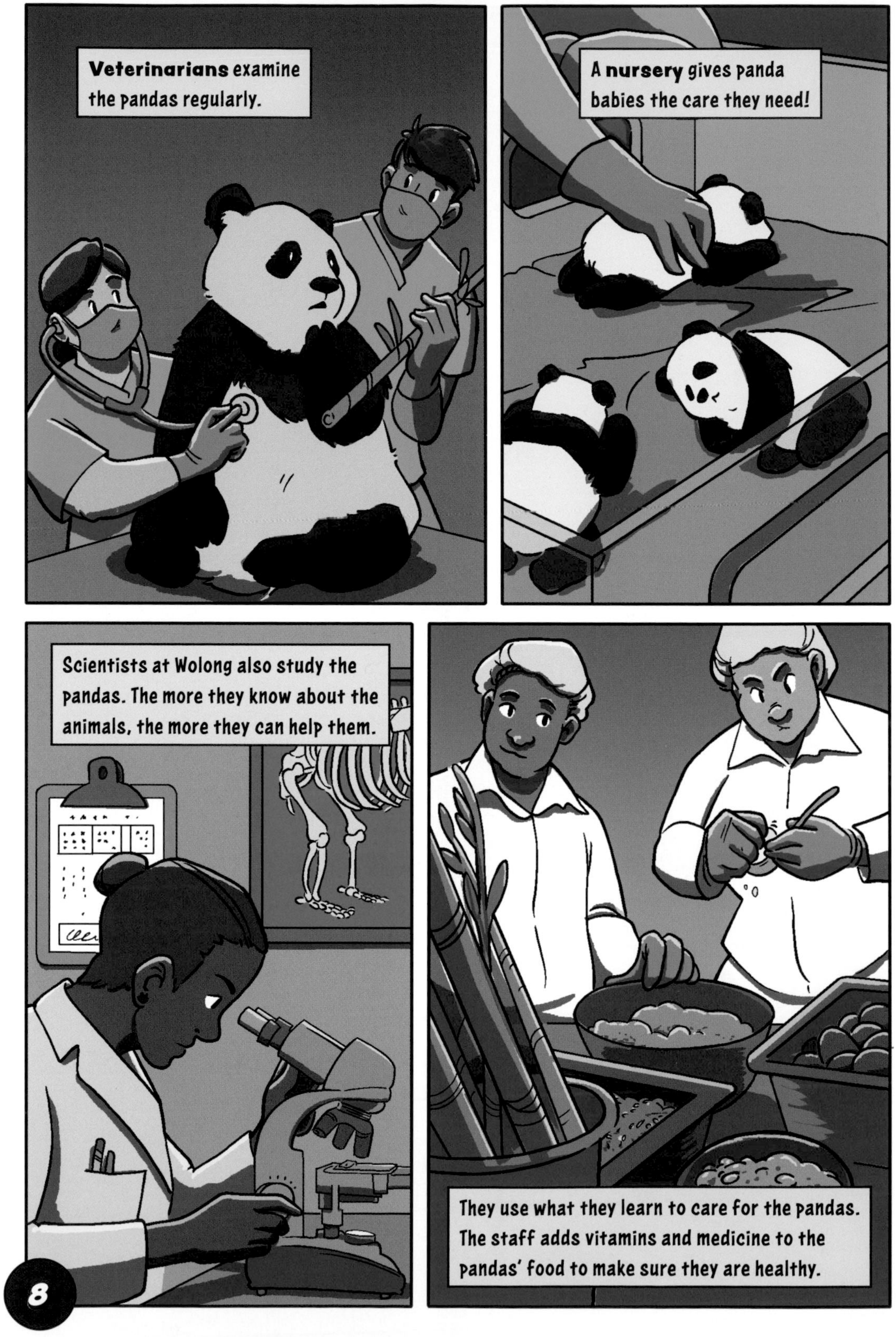
Veterinarians examine the pandas regularly.
A nursery gives panda babies the care they need!
Scientists at Wolong also study the pandas. The more they know about the animals, the more they can help them.
They use what they learn to care for the pandas. The staff adds vitamins and medicine to the pandas' food to make sure they are healthy.

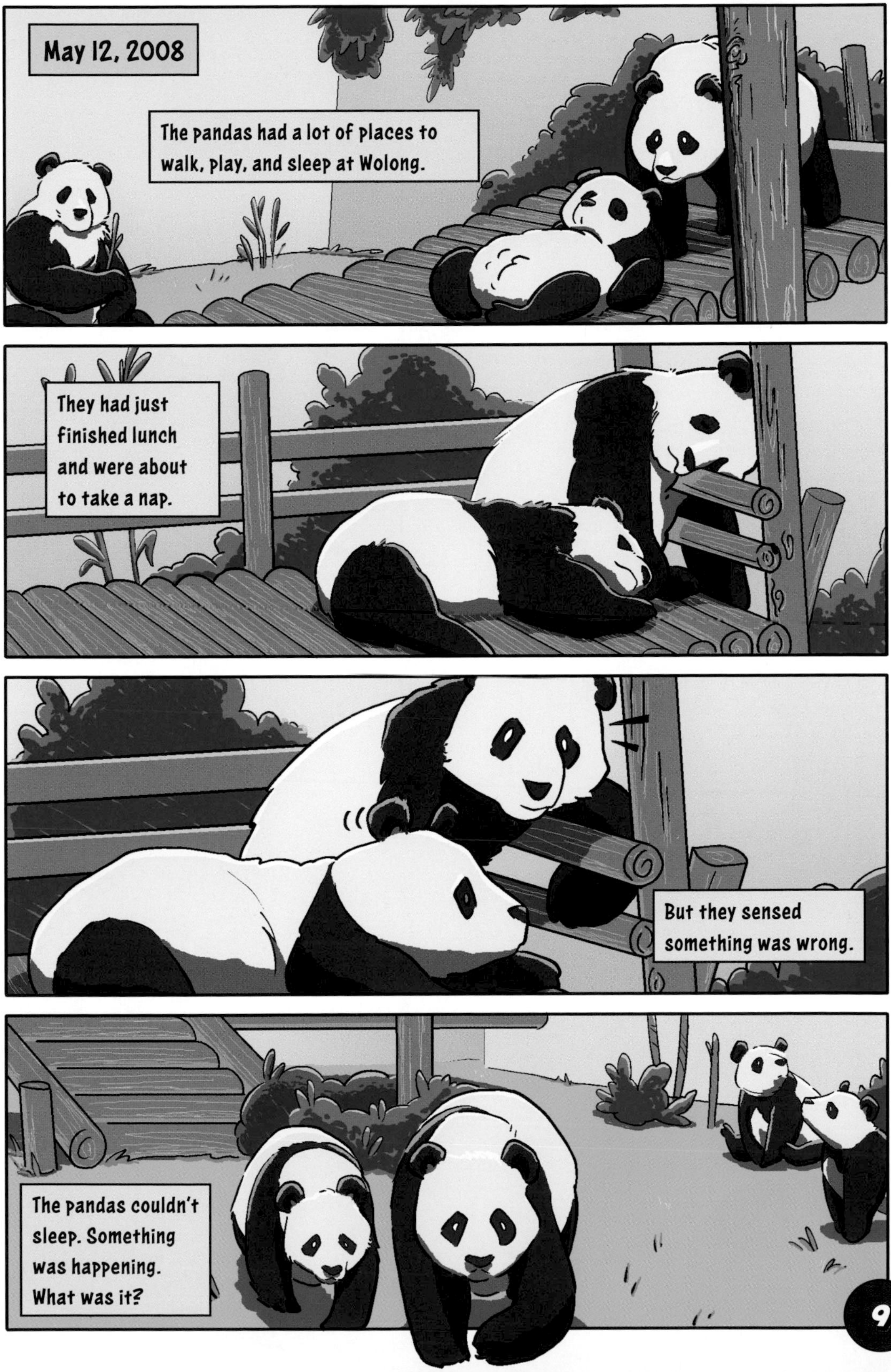
May 12, 2008
The pandas had a lot of places to walk, play, and sleep at Wolong.
They had just finished lunch and were about to take a nap.
But they sensed something was wrong.
The pandas couldn't sleep. Something was happening. What was it?

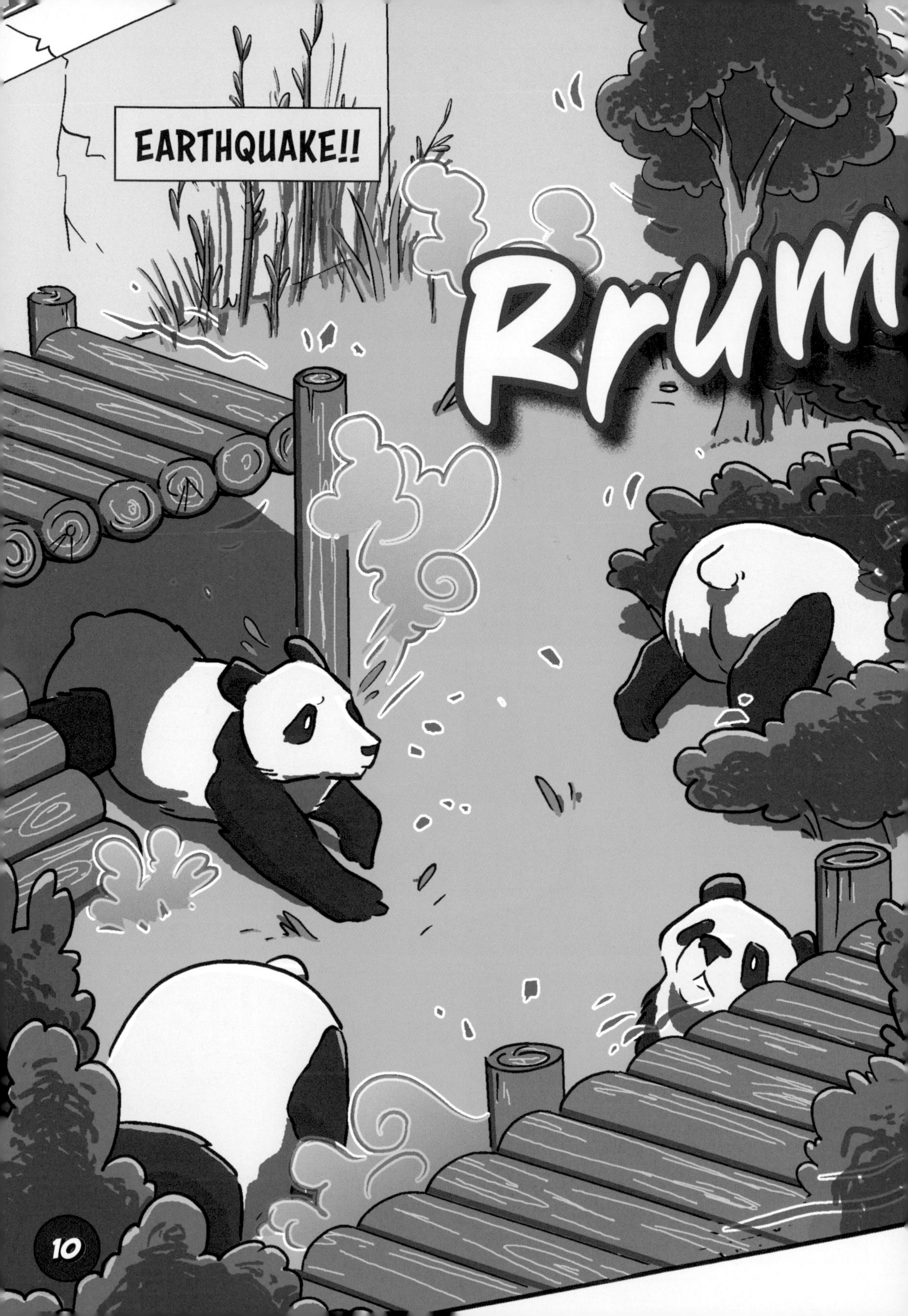
EARTHQUAKE!!
Rrum

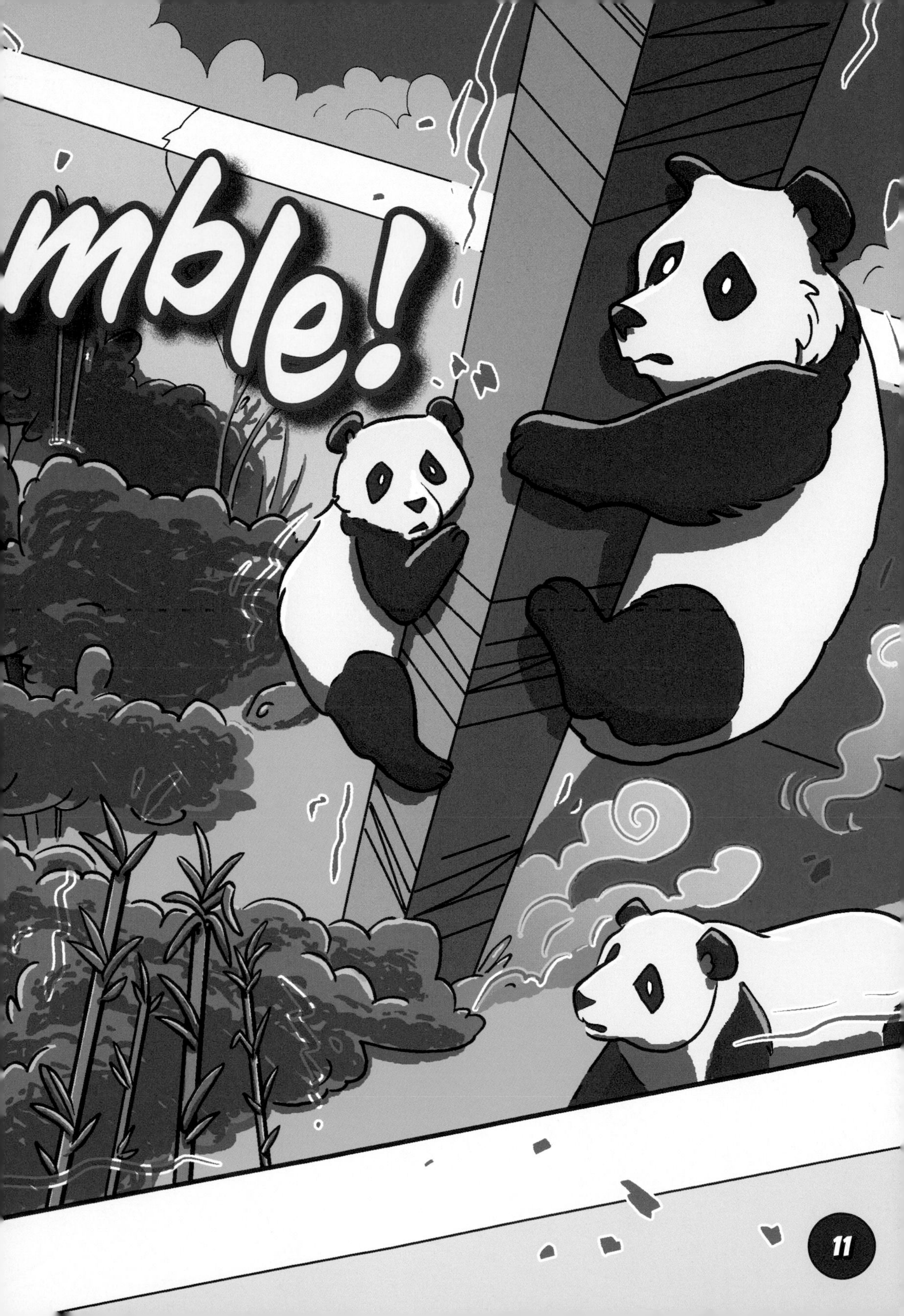
mble!

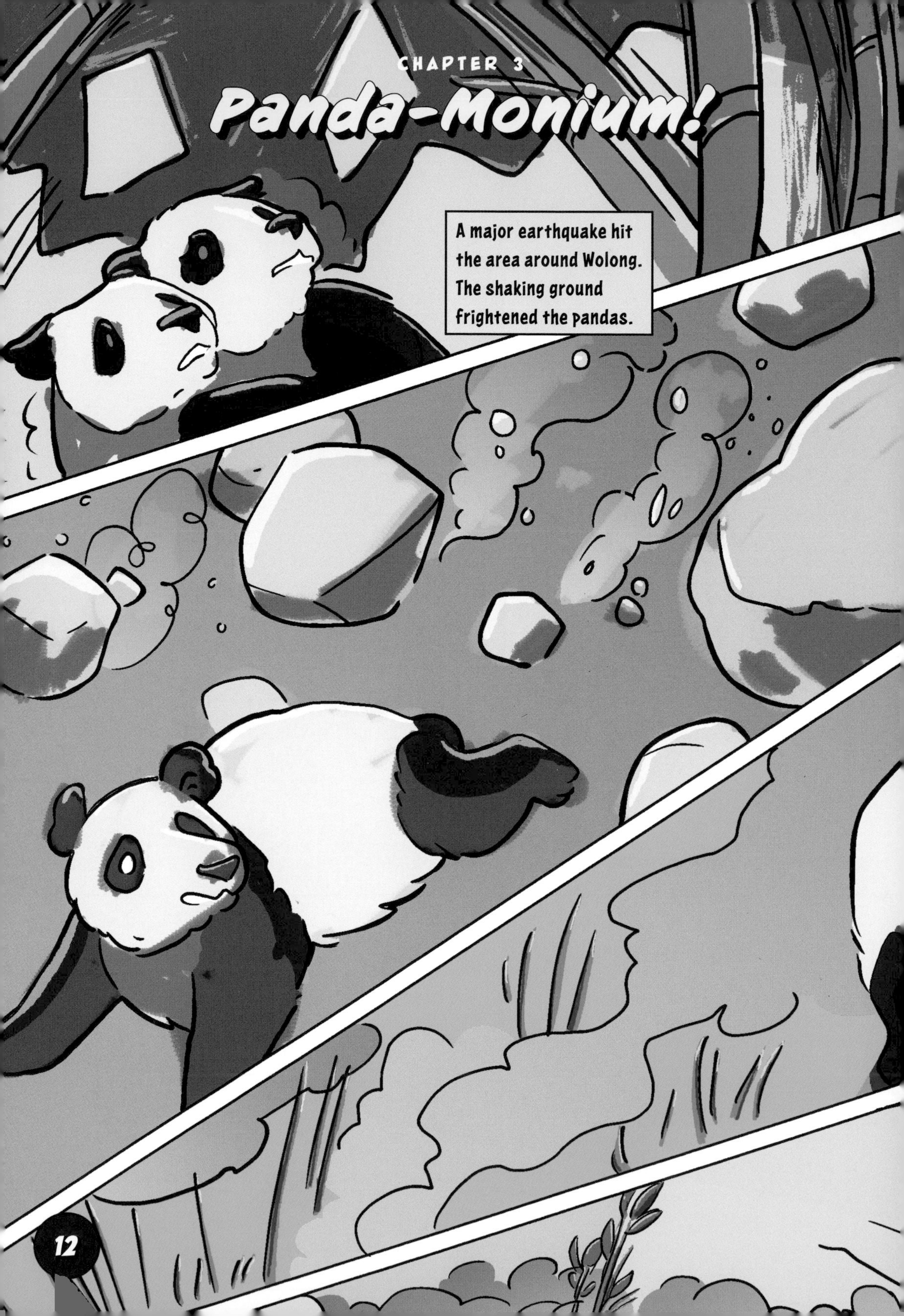
CHAPTER 3
Panda-Monium!
A major earthquake hit the area around Wolong. The shaking ground frightened the pandas.

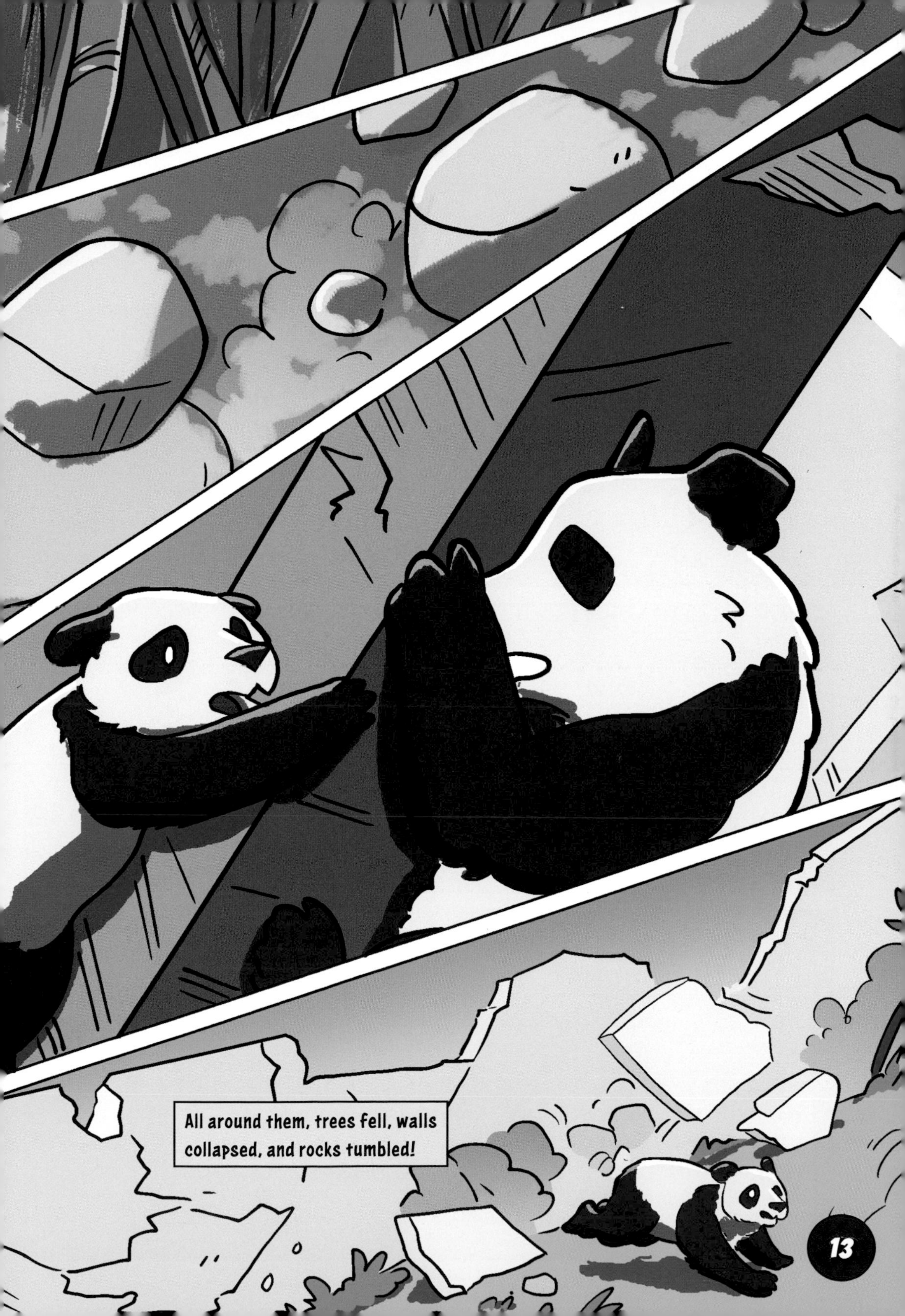
All around them, trees fell, walls collapsed, and rocks tumbled!

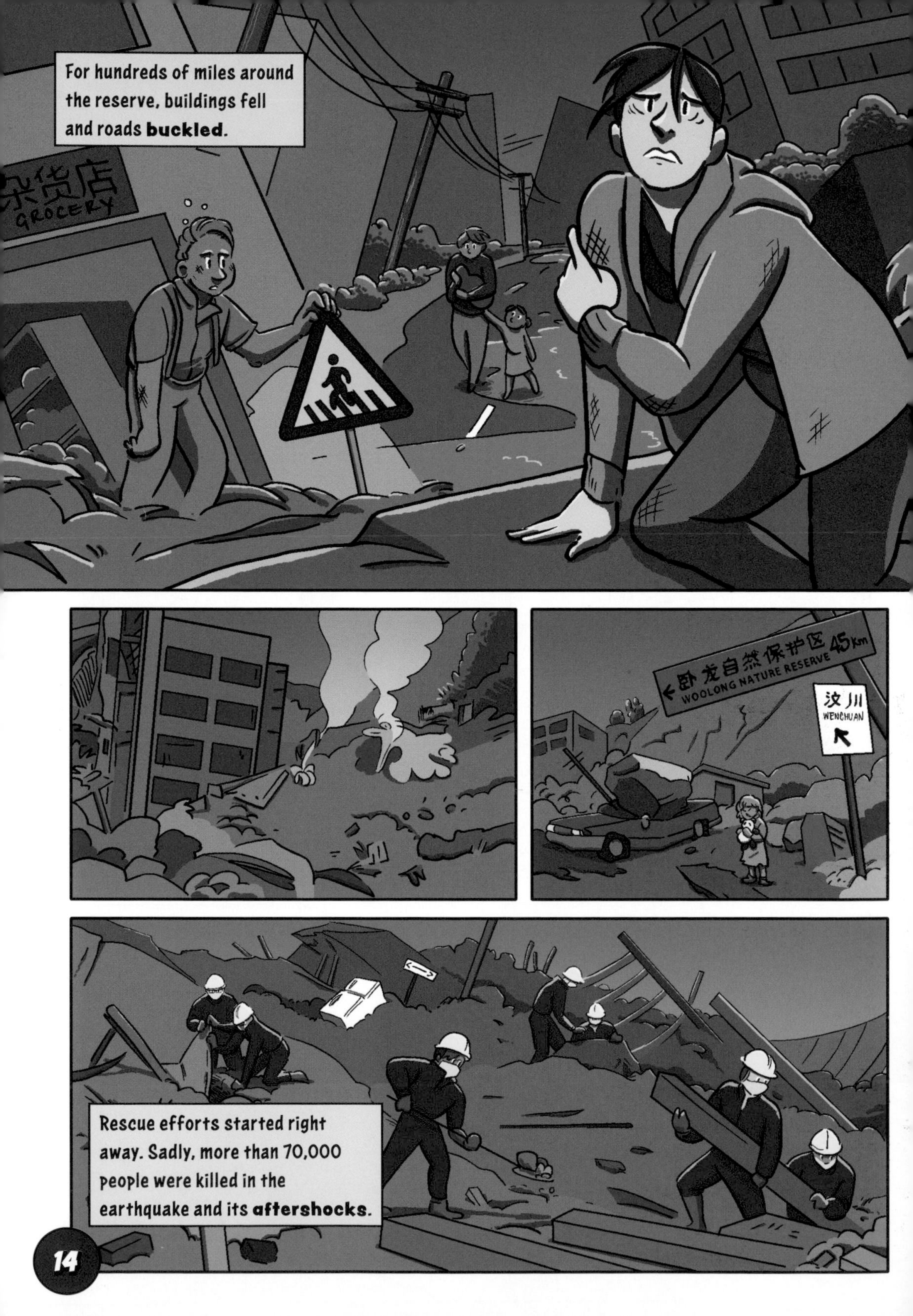
For hundreds of miles around the reserve, buildings fell and roads **buckled**.
杂货店
GROCERY
卧龙自然保护区 45km
WOOLONG NATURE RESERVE
汶川
WENCHUAN
Rescue efforts started right away. Sadly, more than 70,000 people were killed in the earthquake and its **aftershocks**.

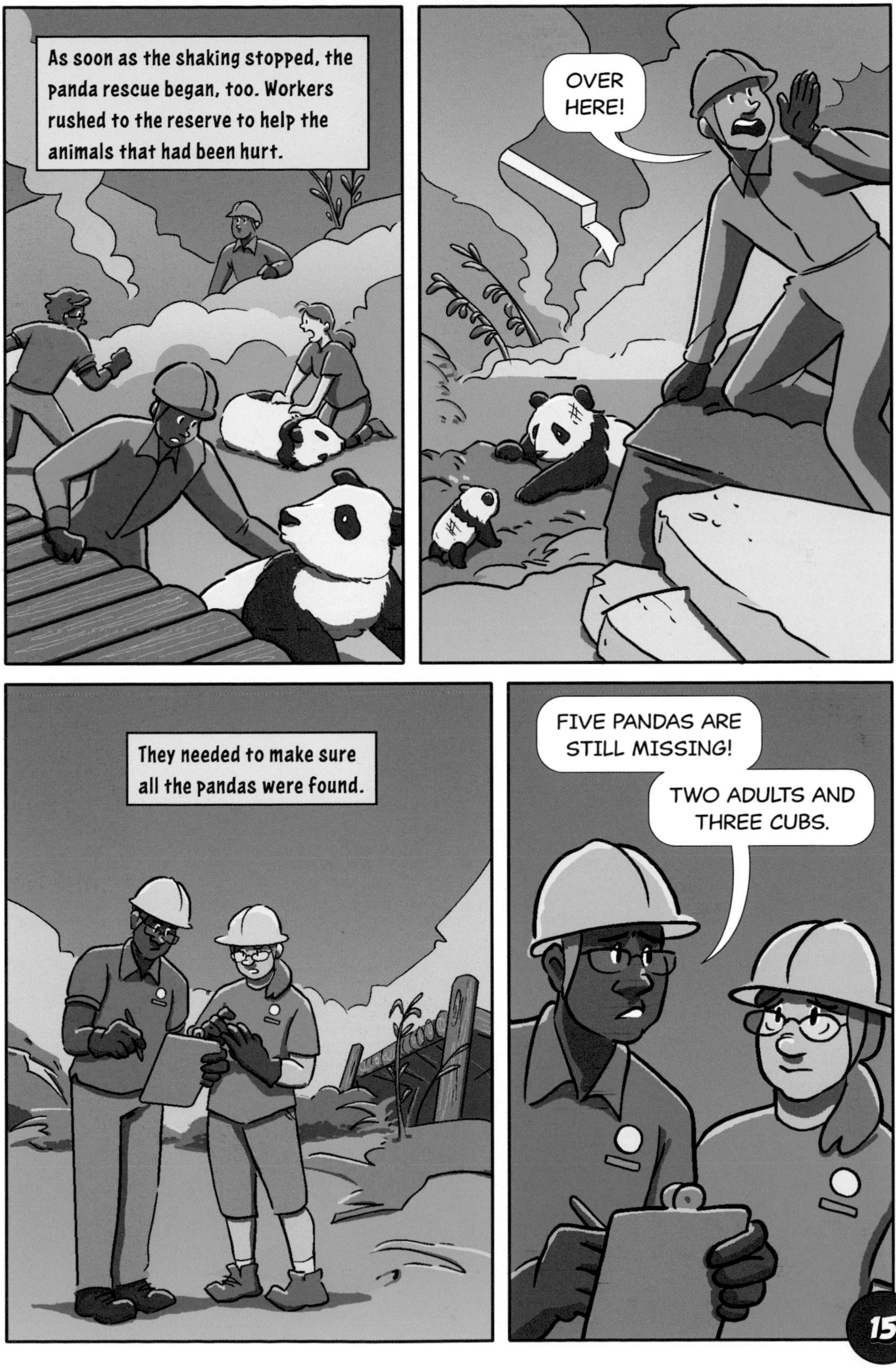
As soon as the shaking stopped, the panda rescue began, too. Workers rushed to the reserve to help the animals that had been hurt.
OVER HERE!
They needed to make sure all the pandas were found.
FIVE PANDAS ARE STILL MISSING!
TWO ADULTS AND THREE CUBS.

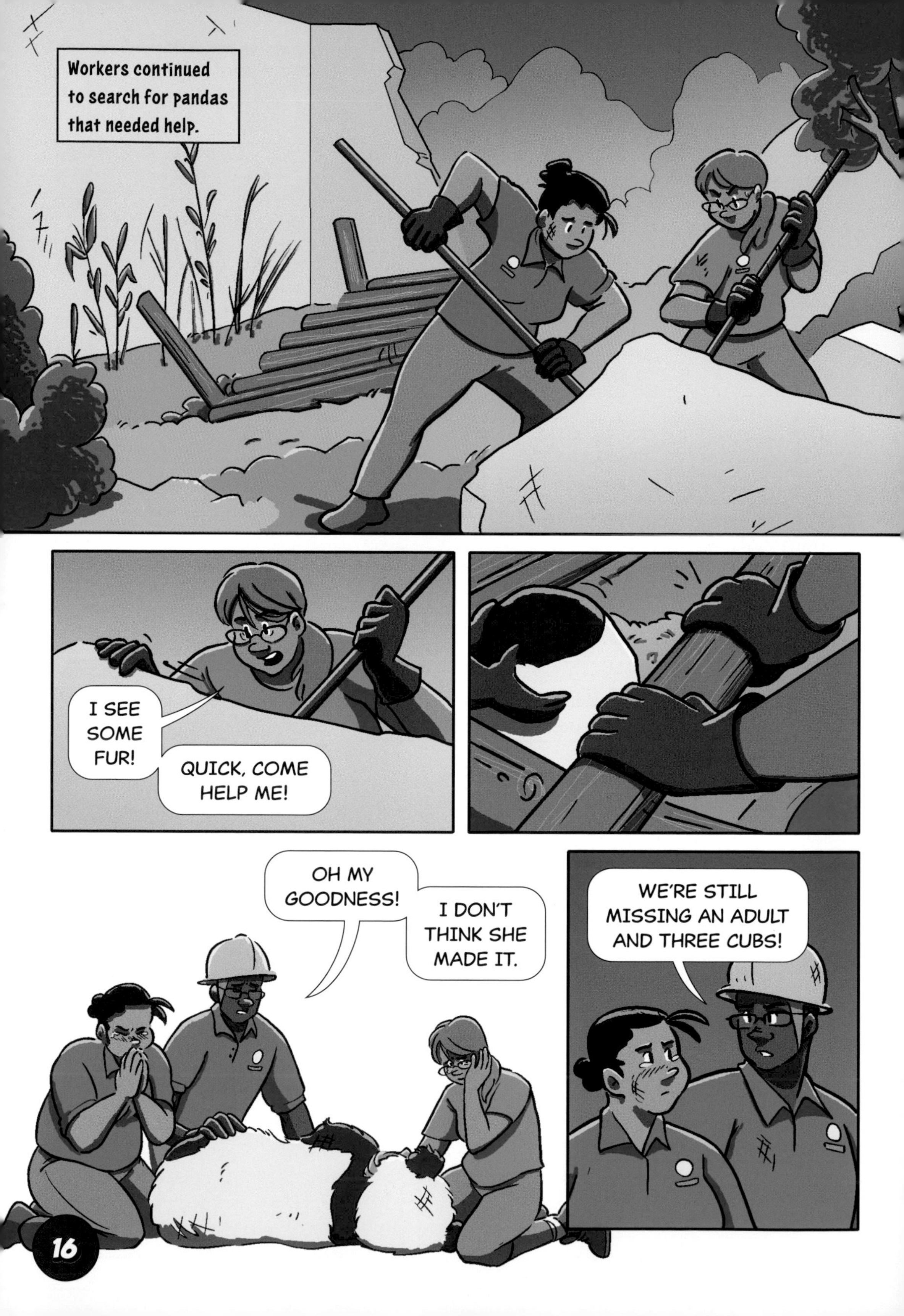
Workers continued to search for pandas that needed help.
I SEE SOME FUR!
QUICK, COME HELP ME!
OH MY GOODNESS!
I DON'T THINK SHE MADE IT.
WE'RE STILL MISSING AN ADULT AND THREE CUBS!

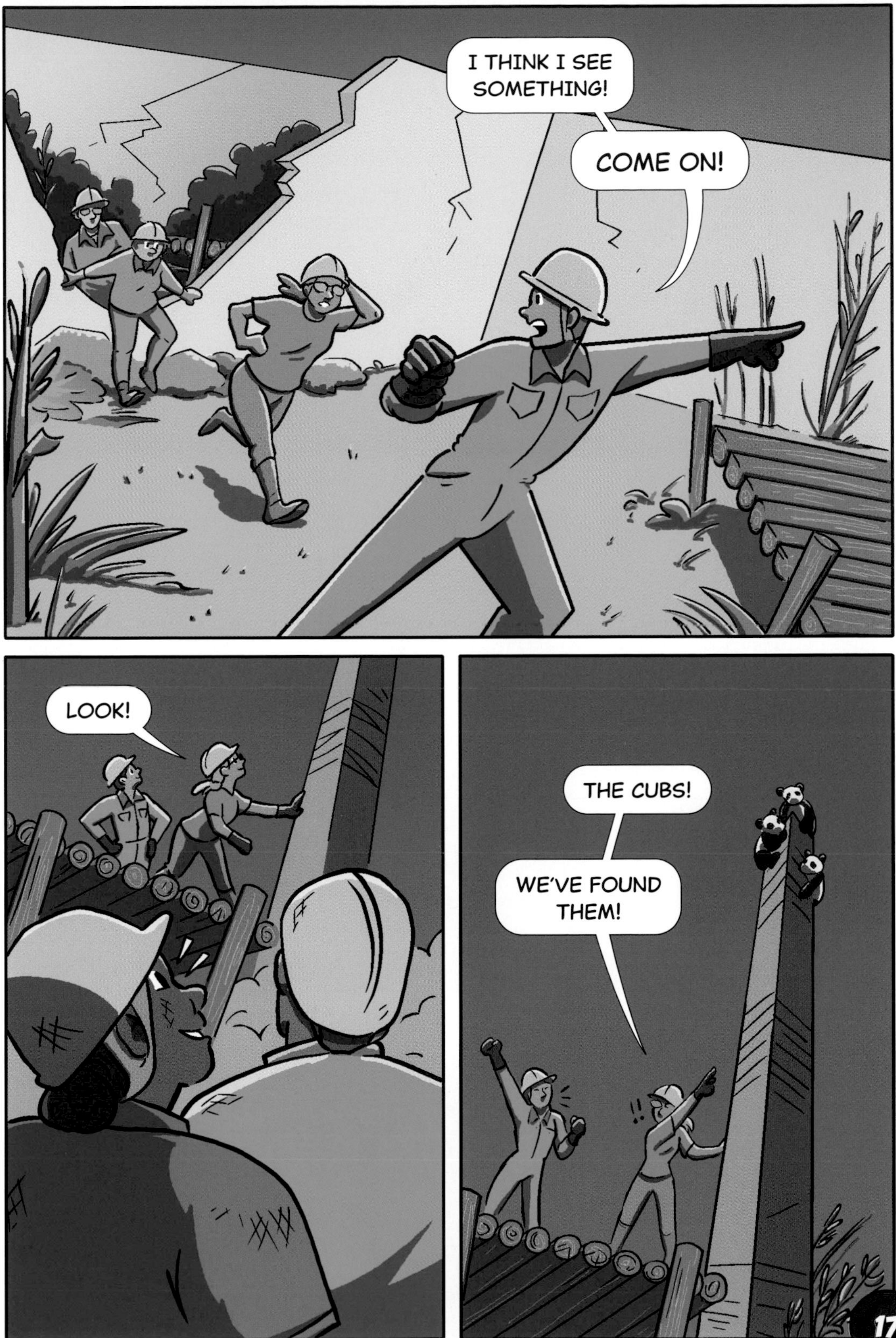
I THINK I SEE SOMETHING!
COME ON!
LOOK!
THE CUBS!
WE'VE FOUND THEM!

CHAPTER 4

Taking Care of the Pandas

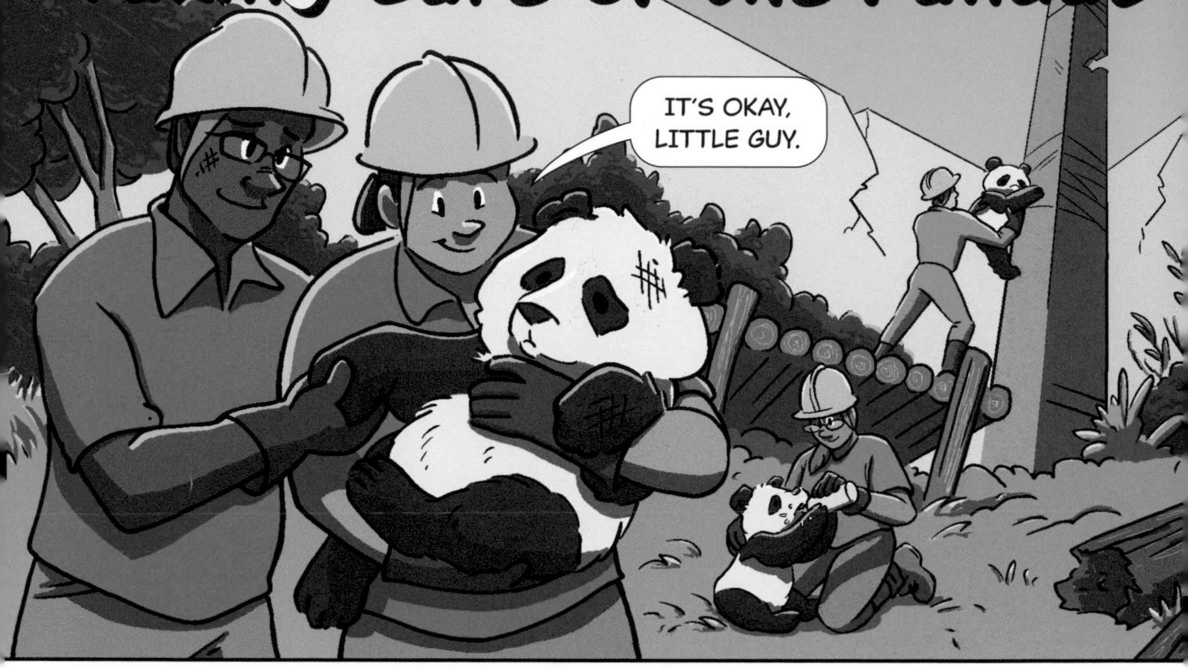
IT'S OKAY, LITTLE GUY.

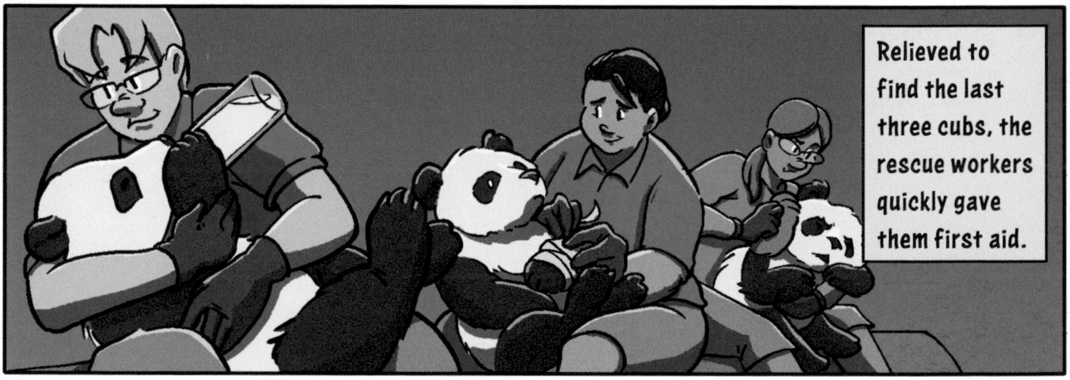
Relieved to find the last three cubs, the rescue workers quickly gave them first aid.

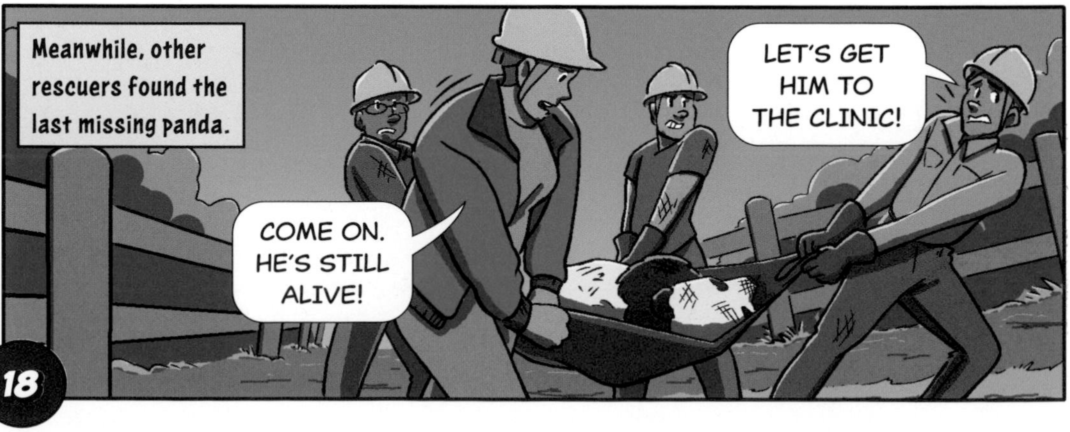
Meanwhile, other rescuers found the last missing panda.
LET'S GET HIM TO THE CLINIC!
COME ON. HE'S STILL ALIVE!

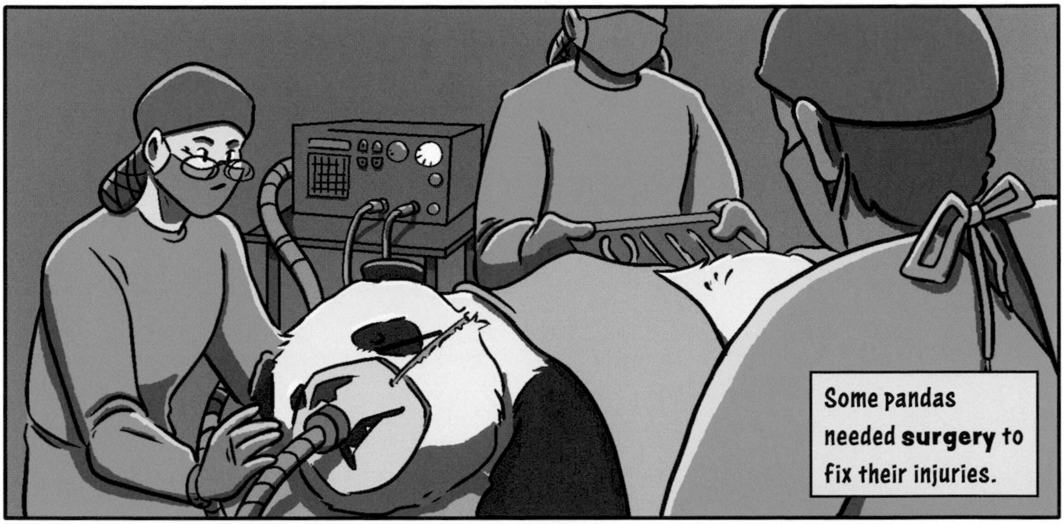
Some pandas needed **surgery** to fix their injuries.

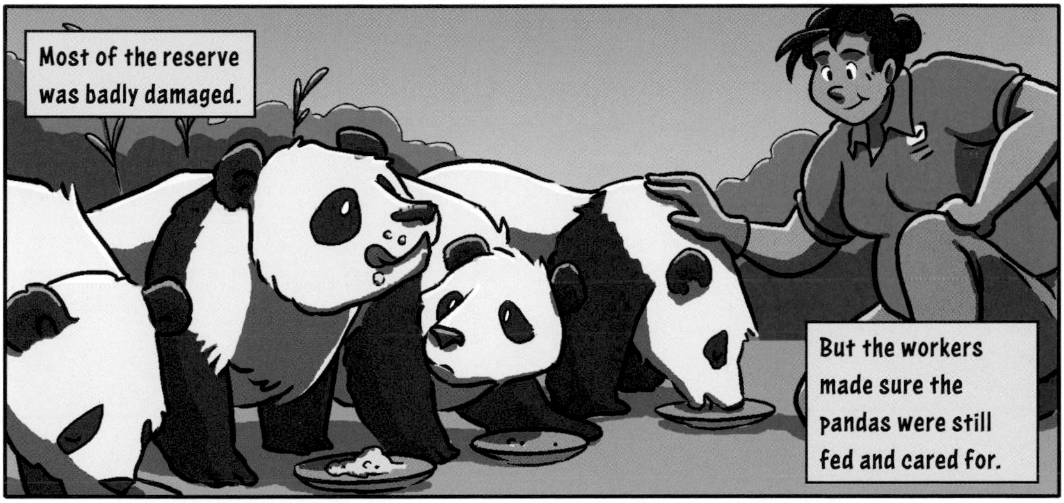
Most of the reserve was badly damaged.
But the workers made sure the pandas were still fed and cared for.

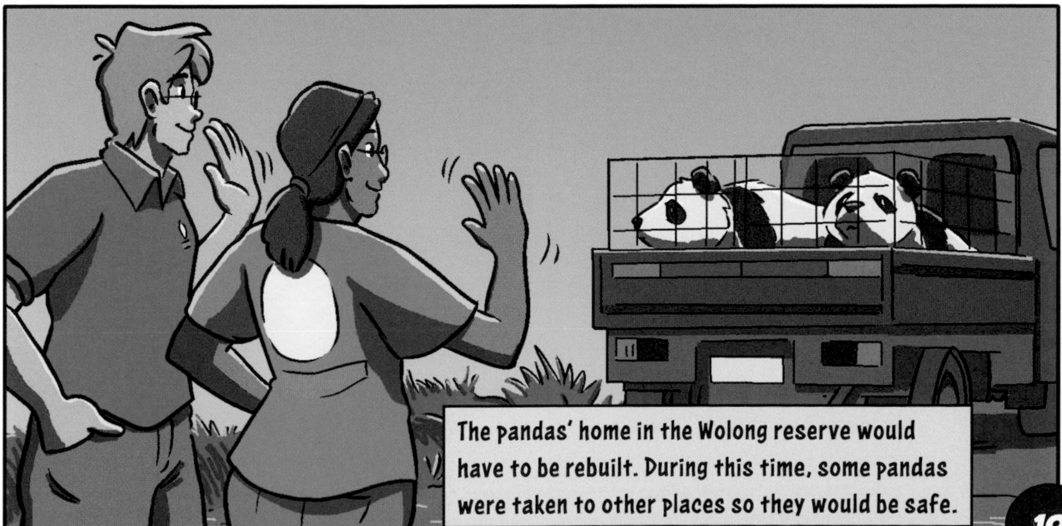
The pandas' home in the Wolong reserve would have to be rebuilt. During this time, some pandas were taken to other places so they would be safe.

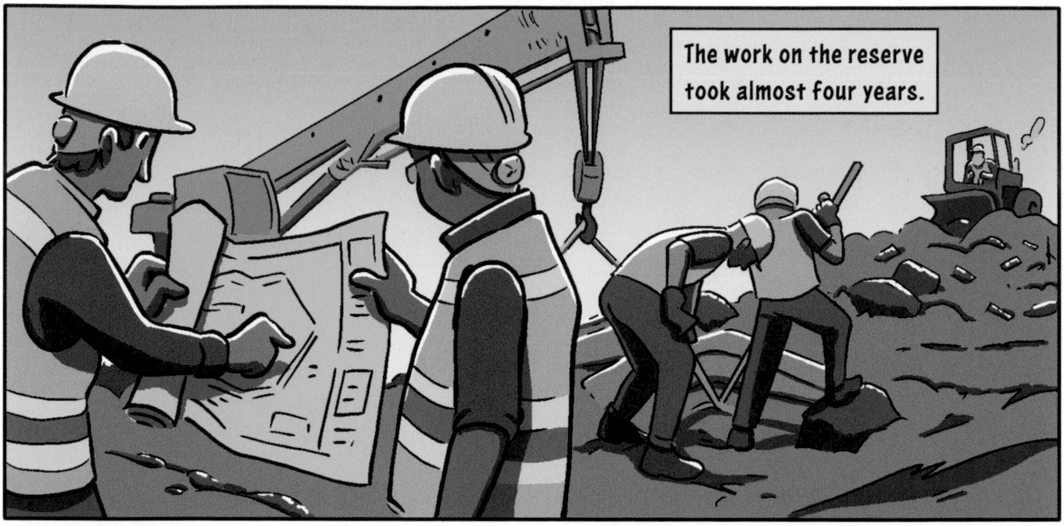
The work on the reserve took almost four years.

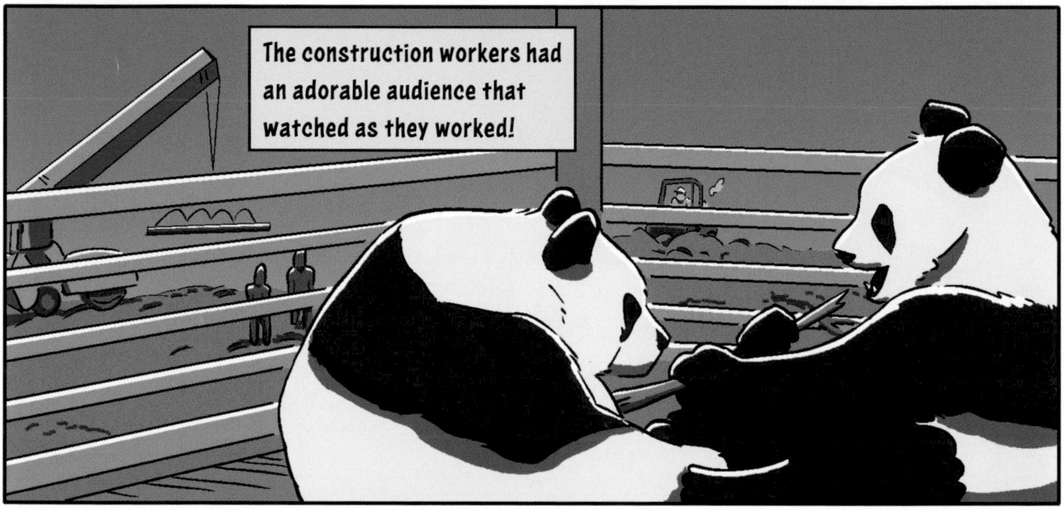
The construction workers had an adorable audience that watched as they worked!

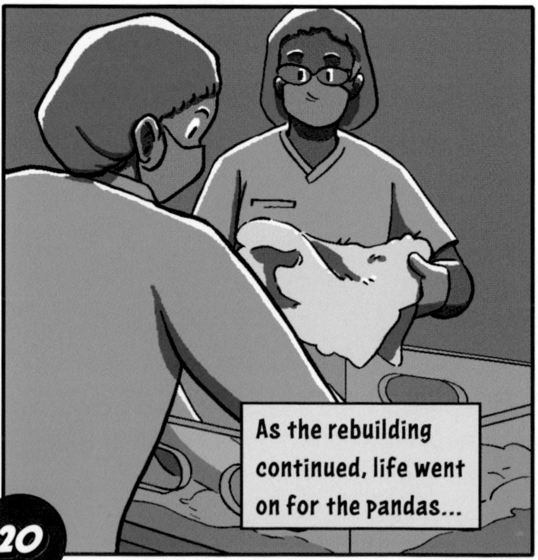
As the rebuilding continued, life went on for the pandas...

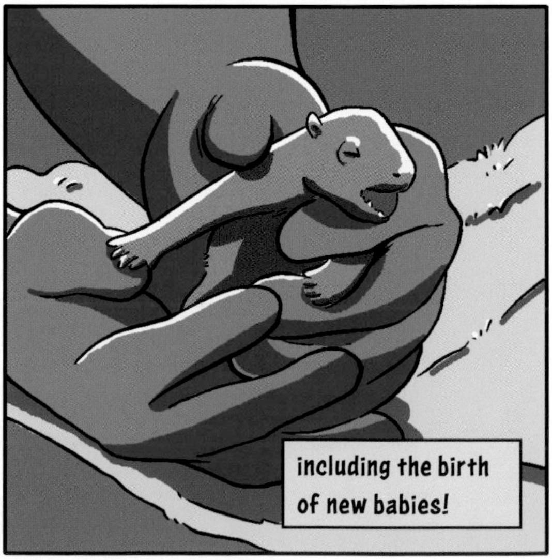
including the birth of new babies!

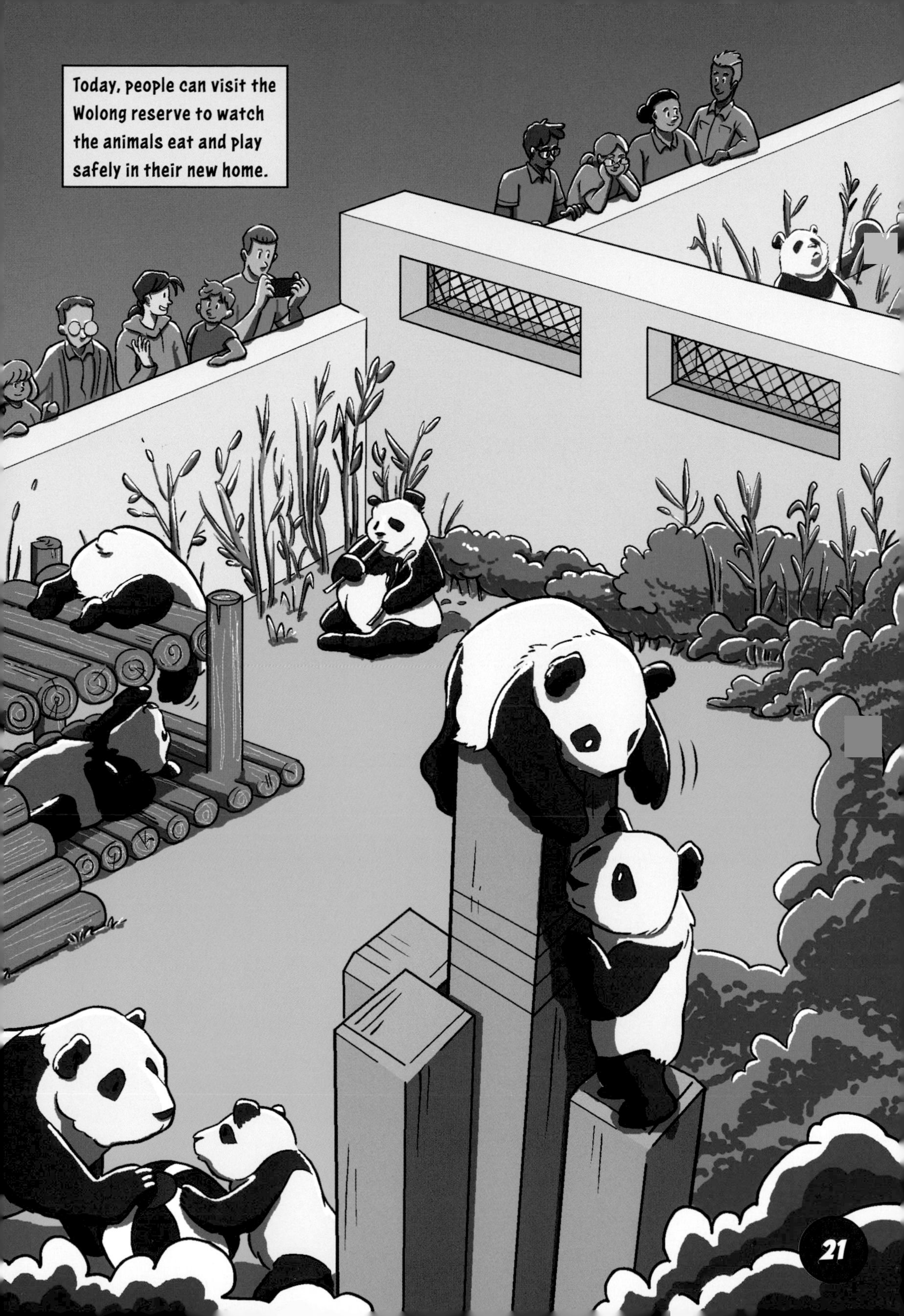
Today, people can visit the Wolong reserve to watch the animals eat and play safely in their new home.

OTHER
EARTHQUAKE RESCUES

JAPAN EARTHQUAKE, 2011

On March 11, 2011, a violent earthquake hit Japan. It measured 8.9 on the **Richter scale**. The earthquake and a **tsunami** that soon followed left millions of people and animals without homes, food, or water. Shortly after the quake, the Japan Earthquake Animal Rescue and Support group (JEARS) was created. Workers searched for lost, trapped, or abandoned animals. They brought food and supplies to shelters where people and their pets were staying.

COSTA RICA EARTHQUAKE, 2009

The earthquake that hit Costa Rica on January 8, 2009, destroyed buildings and caused landslides. Many animal owners were forced to leave their pets as they tried to escape the destruction. Lighthouse Animal Rescue was one of the first rescue organizations in the area after the quake hit. They brought food, water, and medical supplies to trapped and hurt animals.

GLOSSARY

aftershocks smaller earthquakes that happen after a large quake

buckled bent or broke apart

crust Earth's hard outer layer

endangered in danger of dying out

nursery a place where babies are cared for

reserve an area created to give animals and plants a safe and protected home

Richter scale a number system used to indicate the strength of earthquakes; the higher the number, the more powerful the earthquake

surgery a medical procedure inside a body

tectonic plates massive slabs of rock that make up Earth's surface

topple to fall over or collapse

tsunami a huge wave or waves, usually caused by an earthquake, volcanic erruption, or landslide

veterinarians doctors who take care of animals

INDEX

READ MORE

Alderman, Christine Thomas. *Earthquakes (Bolt. Natural Disasters)*. Mankato, MN: Black Rabbit Books, 2021.

McGregor, Harriet. *Flattened by an Earthquake! (Uncharted: Stories of Survival)*. Minneapolis: Bearport Publishing, 2021.

Ventura, Marne. *Earthquakes (Surviving)*. New York: AV2 by Weigl, 2019.

LEARN MORE ONLINE

1. Go to **www.factsurfer.com**
2. Enter "**Panda-Monium**" into the search box.
3. Click on the cover of this book to see a list of websites.